How To Get Ex Back

Time-tested, Effective Hypnotic Techniques That Will
Definitely Get Your Woman To Come Back

*(The Complete Guide To Keeping Your Lover Forever And
Getting Your Ex Back Fast)*

Hilton Durham

TABLE OF CONTENT

Where Did It Go Wrong? 1

Do Not Make These Mistakes 4

Acceptance Of The Reason For The Breakup 11

Know Why You Desire His Return 17

Make Him Interested In You So He Will Pursue You. 34

Recognizing Where Your Relationship Went Wrong 48

How To Get Over Your Obsessions...And Get Over Your Ex 74

The Golden Rule: Do Not Follow Others 93

When An Excellent Relationship Fails 109

You're Either Getting Better Or You Getting Worse 130

You Can Either Win The Battle Or The War 133

These Will Assist You In Winning Them Back And Make You Happier In The Process. 156

Where Did It Go Wrong?

The initial step in mending a relationship is determining the reason for the breakup. Concentrate on the key constraints that may have led to disagreements in the past relationship. At this stage, one should focus on uncovering the most prevalent causes of disputes. Rebuilding a relationship with greater likelihood of happiness can be achieved by identifying the root cause of the breakup.

Without fear or favor, you should be able to identify the source of the problem and devise strategies to prevent future occurrences.

As a future protective measure, it is preferable to concentrate on the general causes of relationship separation after determining the primary cause of the relationship's dissolution. Any individual's subconscious mind must issue a warning if something negative appears to be approaching. Consequently, you will be able to surmount future obstacles.

Understanding the Common Causes of Couples' Separation to Prevent Future Separations

Generally, a couple's separation is brought on by misunderstanding, infidelity, or lack of trust, among other things. In order to develop a healthy relationship, it is essential to recognize each other's weaknesses so that you can provide support. Therefore, this can only be accomplished through effective communication.

Also a primary source of separation is mistrust. When a couple loses trust in one another, it becomes challenging to resolve conflicts. a sensation of dislike begins to germinate. It becomes the source of jealousy, poor behavior, disrespect, and infidelity if it is fostered. When infidelity or cheating is discovered, the likelihood of a relationship ending increases consistently. Consequently, lies steadily begin to defend the act of infidelity. Currently, the relationship is unstable. The act of affection deteriorates, and the blame game is the subsequent occurrence.

Do Not Make These Mistakes

There are certain things you should avoid doing if you want to increase the likelihood that your ex will fall in love with you again. These are errors that could result in your ex leaving you permanently.

Do not create a commotion during or following the breakup.

Do not shriek, become angry, or go insane. Keep your emotions under control. Crying or ranting at him will accomplish nothing. It will only cause him to flee further away from you.

When you act with composure, you tend to equalize the playing field. Try to behave in a way that he probably does not anticipate from you. You will stimulate his curiosity. He will likely be perplexed as to why you do not appear as distraught or as bereft as he anticipated you to be. This will intrigue him, which is a more promising reaction than pity or aversion if you wish to gain him back in the future.

Accept the breakup with as much maturity, grace, and composure as possible. In spite of the pain, he will remember you with admiration and regard if you behave with grace and sophistication.

Do not reveal that you are unhappy.

You likely believe that you must maintain contact with your ex so that he knows you are available. You believe that you must make it simple for him to return to you. According to relationship experts, you must take care not to appear despondent.

If your ex perceives you as desperate or dependent, he will withdraw further. Most men find dependent women unattractive. Do not call or text him as if you have nothing better to do with your time. Even if this were true, you should not tell him.

Do not beseech or plead with him to reconsider the relationship.

Do not implore him to stay with you. You will lose respect and dignity for yourself.

Do not imply that you are unable to survive without him. This will not convince him to accept you back. Simply, he will perceive you as apprehensive, feeble, and unattractive.

You do not wish to engage your man in a game of pity. Do you want your relationship to be restored if he changes his mind out of compassion? Love, trust, respect, appreciation, comprehension, and a desire for companionship are superior and more robust relationship building blocks. You do not desire a relationship built primarily on sympathy.

If your ex decides not to break up with you out of pity, you may have to face severe consequences. Over time, he will likely regret making this choice. He will eventually realize that he accepted your return for the wrong reasons. He may even hold you responsible. He will likely want to leave again.

If you cry, scream, or threaten to do something terrible if your ex refuses to reconcile, you are essentially holding him for ransom. You are manipulating and emotionally blackmailing others. If he agrees to reconcile with you, he will likely develop resentment and anger. There is a high likelihood that he will break up with you once more.

Do not permit him to stroll over you.

Do not give up everything to restore the relationship.

You may believe you can gain back your boyfriend by giving in to all of his demands. You will have a rough journey. Do not sacrifice your wants, needs, values, and objectives in order to get back together with your former. If you allow him to use you as a doormat, he will likely lose all respect for you. YOU are at risk of losing respect for yourself. A relationship lacking respect is unlikely to succeed.

For your relationship to succeed, you must be both willing and able to resolve your differences. Both parties should be prepared to compromise. If only one party is willing to negotiate, the relationship is imbalanced. It will ultimately fail.

Interrupt all forms of communication with your ex-partner temporarily.

This period is referred to by relationship experts as the no contact rule. The rule states that you must cease all forms of contact with your ex. This encompasses every form of communication. Do not contact. Never communicate. Sending personal communications through Facebook is prohibited. Avoid communicating with him via Twitter and other similar platforms. Do not even go out with shared companions in the hopes of running into him.

You and your ex will be extremely emotional immediately following the breakup. You will find it difficult to make rational or well-considered decisions. Eliminate all communication with one another. This will serve to soothe your emotions. This will help you evaluate your respective positions rationally.

The rule of no contact will also give you time to recover. Break-ups are difficult.

You harm one another and incline to view one another with contempt. You must afford time for tempers to cool. You need time to reflect. You need healing time. If you attempt reconciliation without taking time to make significant realizations, you will encounter the same old problems. You will once again face the same divisive issues.

You must permit time to pass. The time apart will allow you to examine the breakup with a more objective and constructive perspective. Only by giving each other space to breathe can you hope to be able to communicate without intense emotions. Then and only then will you be able to make the necessary repairs.

The no contact rule will also assist you in reevaluating your life. It provides a sense of perspective. It allows you to make positive changes to your lifestyle. This is crucial. If you ultimately determine you want your ex back, the time apart should have made you a happier and more attractive woman.

ACCEPTANCE OF THE REASON FOR THE BREAKUP

Throughout the centuries, innumerable works of art and songs have attempted to capture the anguish associated with a breakup. It is a topic whose universality resonates with a large number of individuals who have at some point experienced the heartbreaking tragedy of loving another person and then being spurned. Nevertheless, despite the existence of these works and the near-ubiquity of their subject matter, nothing can prepare a person for the pain and even trauma associated with breaking up with someone they have loved and continue to adore.

As a matter of fact, coping with a breakup is almost always an individual experience that cannot be standardized. We each have our own methods for dealing with similar situations. What is not uncommon, however, is the realization that many people reach after a breakup: despite everything that has occurred in the past, they cannot exist without their exes by their side.

It's unfortunate that it takes an emotionally taxing experience like a breakup for one to realize the depth and breadth of one's affection for another. This lends credence to the age-old adage that you can only appreciate someone's value once they have left your existence.

Better, more resilient

Understand that breakups are not the conclusion of relationships despite this. In fact, regarded differently, they may be precisely what your relationship requires to become stronger and more resilient in the future. However, this is only feasible if you were able to regain your ex's affection and love after the breakup.

If you ever want your ex to return to your life, you must be utterly certain of two things: first, is this something you truly desire? And secondly, what was the true reason you and your ex-partner decided to break up in the first place?

The first query assumes several conditions. It is presumed that you remain emotionally invested in your ex-partner. Why else would you even consider reconciling with him or her? Bringing your ex back into your life indicates that you appreciate his or her qualities, as well as the time and memories you shared together. Given these circumstances, is it in your best interests to rekindle your romance? It would be helpful to have a list of pros and cons to guide your decision-making.

Improving matters for the future

The second question requires a comprehensive comprehension of the reasons why your relationship failed. It is necessary to determine the precise cause of your separation in order to design a plan that will result in reconciliation. Who initiated the separation? You were either the dumper or the dumpee. What, if anything, did you do or say that may have contributed to the unfortunate course of events?

What prompted you to discard your ex, if it was you who did so? What did your ex-partner do or say that prompted you to conclude it's best to end the relationship? Were other individuals involved? Was your divorce a mutual decision?

In any case, if you decide to pursue your ex again, you should be willing to make adjustments or concessions to make things better in the future. And if you are certain that this is precisely what you must do, then by all means engage in a battle for it. The subsequent chapters detail the actions and mechanisms you must implement to get your ex back within a month.

Do you want immediate, free access to my most recent Kindle books?

Enter your name and e-mail address below to gain FREE IMMEDIATE ACCESS to my exclusive e-mail newsletter and receive my most recent Kindle novels for

FREE directly to your inbox! You will be able to obtain them directly from Amazon or your Kindle device and begin reading them in a matter of seconds, at no cost.

KNOW WHY YOU DESIRE HIS RETURN

If you followed the advice in the previous section, you should understand why your ex is no longer in your life. You should have been straightforward and truthful with yourself about why the relationship is now over. Now please answer the following question: why do you want him back? What are the characteristics that make you want this person back in your life? Ensure that the reason or reasons you want him back are beneficial and will improve your life. So many women have attempted to regain a man for the wrong reasons. I am aware that this is an archaic way of thinking, but genuine affection for this person should be one of the primary, if not the only, reason you desire a reconciliation.

Do you mourn his voice, touch, personality, and the way he makes you feel in general when he's around? If you answered affirmatively to the majority or all of these questions, you are on the correct path. You should not want your former back because he's wealthy, the father of your child, the only man you've ever dated, or for any other pitfalls like these. If your reason for wanting him back is not genuine, even if you do get him back, the relationship will likely not last, and if it does, you will likely not be satisfied. Remember that I stated at the outset of the book that you should be in a relationship with someone who fulfills your relationship goals?

It's time to ask yourself, "What am I missing?" if you weren't genuinely happy while you were with him, and part of that was because he treated you poorly. Only you are aware of the reasons why you desire his return. Remember what you have just read.

Does The Game of Jealousy Work?

This is a topic that I have both experienced and read extensively about. Some women believe that if their ex-boyfriend sees or hears them with another man, this will attract their attention and ultimately convince them to return. Permit me to share my real-world perspective on the "make him jealous" concept. So, can you get your ex-boyfriend back by simply courting or being around another man? The response is... It depends on how you ended your relationship and what type of man your ex is. Obviously, if the relationship ended due to your infidelity and he left you, you would not want him to believe that you are involved with any man if you are attempting to win him back. If your boyfriend dumped you for another woman, employing the jealousy card is unlikely to be effective. In my opinion, the "make him jealous" strategy will only work if he ended the relationship out of dread of marriage because he felt pressured to take things to the next level and feared commitment. When you believe that he truly loves you but is too afraid to commit to you and instead chooses to leave rather than confront his fears. This is when the envious individual may realize that you are not worth losing. The idea of another man having a woman as exceptional as you can rapidly alleviate his commitment anxiety.

Other than this reason, I would generally avoid making him envious, and I would proceed with caution even in this situation. This is because people today are wilder than ever before. It seems like every day there is a news story about a man or woman who snaps and does something incredibly foolish out of jealousy. You may be reading this and imagining that your ex would never harm you or do something insane. Remember that in many instances, the person you least expect to do something is the one who actually does it.

To conclude, when attempting to get your ex back, you should be cautious about playing the jealously game. It is possible, but remember everything discussed in this section.

The Reality Behind Giving Him Space

Numerous relationship experts recommend that women grant their ex-boyfriends space. This essentially signifies that you will cease all communication for a period of time. The concept underlying this technique is straightforward. You do not call, text, or even email your ex regarding anything. This should make your ex ponder what you're doing and why you haven't reached out to him. He will eventually be overcome with curiosity and make contact with you. This is your chance to repair the relationship. However, does this method work? Honestly, this is very similar to the entire jealously strategy. It depends on the circumstances and the type of man your ex-boyfriend is. Giving your ex complete space will only be effective if you believe he will miss you. It will be successful if you are confident that whatever he is doing cannot compare to being with you. If you wish to use the space thing to retrieve him, you must sincerely believe this. If a man believes that his current activity is preferable to being with you, granting him space will not work. It will drastically reduce your prospects of obtaining his return. The time has come for you to ask yourself, "Is there anything or anyone better than being with me?" and "Do I believe he will miss me in time?"

Before deciding to employ this method, you should carefully consider the nature of your previous relationship. Consider the manner in which the relationship terminated. Even though some experts recommend giving your ex some space, if you are sincere about getting him back, you may not need to do so. Thoroughly assess the circumstance.

Clever strategies to regain your ex-boyfriend

If you're looking for ways to win back your ex-boyfriend, you're in the correct place. Your ex will adapt to a new relationship, despite the fact that it may seem difficult to alter him. You will require a large number of victims and a great deal of patience to make the new relationship succeed. Here are ten cunning ways to convince your ex-boyfriend to reconcile.

Be persistent: Your ex-boyfriend will be the first to recognize your persistence in regards to your relationship. It is in our nature to want to keep objects we value. Therefore, you must cease making the same errors and fix the damage you've caused. One effective strategy is to avoid all contact with him. You will silently persist to get your ex-boyfriend back if you are persistent.

Don't be a doormat. It is a common error to attempt to entice your ex back by lavishing him with affection. It indicates desperation. You are not in a dire situation; your ex already knows that you love and care for him, so keep things simple and let him decide for himself. Remember that pleading and pitiful behavior are not appealing.

If you have been ignoring issues in your relationship, your chances of reconciling are limited. However, this does not imply that you can never win him back. Every day, numerous women reconcile with their exes. The majority lose their ex because they have not resolved the underlying issues that led to the separation. So, take the time to determine why it took so long to reunite.

Don't hurt his emotions

If you wish to reconcile with your ex, you must recognize that you cannot impose your will on the relationship. You must assume responsibility and act strategically to avoid hurting his emotions. The breakup has left your ex-boyfriend feeling wounded, so you must avoid hurting his feelings further. Although he may be in need of affection, it is impossible to control another person's emotions. This article will help you comprehend why your ex-boyfriend may not be ready to rekindle his relationship with you.

It is understandable that the relationship has deteriorated, but you must exercise patience. Relationship issues require time and resolution. Attempt not to hurt his feelings as he undergoes a significant transition. During this time, reach out as a friend and encourage him to open up to you. Even if he does not respond immediately, he will likely appreciate your efforts.

You may be compelled to flatter your ex when you're attempting to win back your ex-boyfriend, but a bruised ego is unlikely to work. A wounded ego can lead to self-doubt and unfavorable behavior. Here are a few methods for mending your wounded ego. You may be compelled to send your ex a text message out of boredom or guilt.

Honor his boundaries. If you have acted in an unromantic manner or hurt your ex's feelings in any way, it is essential to apologize and make amends. Your ex may feel terrible and miss you if you disregard his limits. If you hurt his emotions, he may even feel remorseful. If you cannot make restitution, he will not even want to reconcile.

Induce loss dread

Typically, breakups are agonizing. Instead of venting online, speak with your closest friends and attempt to put yourself in his shoes. Avoid spreading falsehoods and sending mean-spirited text messages. Even if your intentions are pure, these actions will only serve to make your ex-boyfriend feel worse. So, how can you win back your ex-boyfriend?

The first step in regaining your ex-boyfriend is to alter your lifestyle. This is simpler said than done, but it will be extremely beneficial. Spending time apart from your ex will allow you to evaluate whether your relationship is still worth fighting for. It will be difficult to end the phone conversation, but you must prioritize making adjustments in your life. Induce loss apprehension in your ex.

You should determine whether you can resolve the issues you had together. Were there any problems that led to the split? Can they be resolved? If you do not, you may face larger conflicts in the future. If this is not the case, you should wait a few months. Hopefully, they'll discover another cause to strive for! You can then begin the process of rekindling the relationship with loss apprehension.

Induce fear of loss as the most effective psychological strategy to get your ex-boyfriend back requires significant effort. This strategy is known as "dumpsters remorse" and relies on a confluence of factors converging at the right moment. By concentrating on these factors, you can reach your objective. Your ex will feel regret.

Do not succumb to desperation

If you are in a relationship and desperately want your ex-boyfriend back, you may place yourself in a precarious position. Even though your ex may want to reconcile, you should be aware that he will not do so unless he feels like it. You should avoid acting out of desperation and remain hopeful for positive news. Instead, you should act strategically and refrain from acting in desperation. You can rest assured that your ex will not feel like he has control over you if you take this action. Consider that he may be seeking a more suitable partner for someone else.

First and foremost, you must recuperate. You must overcome your divorce. This could be a sign of desperation if you are despondent or fear losing him. In such a situation, it is advisable to seek professional assistance. If your relationship has ended due to issues of trust, this may be the best option. Additionally, you should care for yourself. Do not spend time brooding and dwelling on the past. Instead, you should clean your apartment and purchase yourself a gift.

Similarly, do not attempt to persuade your ex-boyfriend to return by lavishing him with affection. Indulging in desperation indicates that you are no longer committed to reconciling. If your ex-boyfriend knows that you still love him, there is no sense in reminding him. It will only drive him away and make you appear desperate.

Don't make him feel like he's lost eternally

If you are going through a divorce, do not fall into the trap of believing that he is gone permanently. Breakups can cause a variety of feelings, including hopelessness, depression, and despair. The last thing you desire is to cause your ex additional pain. However, if you text your ex in an attempt to rekindle the relationship, make sure to text him subtly and with only positive intentions. There is no need to rekindle feelings that could entice your ex-boyfriend to rekindle the relationship.

You should not email your ex-boyfriend about your breakup. If you don't mention the separation, he won't notice your texts, so keep your conversations positive. While you may mourn your ex-boyfriend, don't give him the impression that you're trying to win him back. It will ultimately backfire and destroy the no contact period for both of you.

Do not make your ex-boyfriend believe that you are an idiot. You have destroyed his life by worrying about him and tolerating his poor behavior in order to feel important and desired. This only gives him the impression that you are frantic, leading to a downward spiral. Remember that a healthy relationship requires both parties to make reasonable requests. Therefore, if you do not make reasonable demands of your companion, he will move on.

Your ex-boyfriend will likely have some sentiments for you after a breakup, but they are extremely unlikely to remember you. Therefore, you should respect his space and allow him to find contentment elsewhere. If you maintain contact with him, you will inevitably encounter reminders of your relationship. It will only increase his longing for you. Additionally, you will mourn him when he is absent.

MAKE HIM INTERESTED IN YOU SO HE WILL PURSUE YOU.

Getting an ex to pursue you is essential if you want him to return. It is common knowledge among the majority of women who like to research or read about males.

Well, if you pause and give it some thought, getting another person to pursue you romantically is not an easy feat. But I intend to change that with the following advice.

Remember, when it comes to bringing an ex back, the woman who is less emotional and more logical tends to win in the end. Now, I'm not saying that being emotional can never be advantageous, but it can work against you if you're attempting to attract someone's pursuit.

Do not develop an emotional texting style

This individual sends double texts with excessively emotional messages such as 'are you there?', 'why aren't you answering me?', 'ANSWER ME', and 'Fine, don't bother talking to me ever again'.

I want you to see how tragic this individual appears. She initially sent a text message to inquire if the other person was present. As time passed and she received no response, her anger grew. If your ex considers you to be an emotional texter, he will be less likely to pursue you because there will be nothing left for him to experience the thrill of the pursuit with.

Getting an ex-boyfriend to pursue you again requires perseverance, some luck, and a bit of strategy. In this case, there are two principles. The patience when there is no contact and the patience when there is contact.

A period during which you have no contact with your ex. Typically lasting 30 days on average. Consequently, you are not permitted to contact him during the no contact period, nor are you permitted to contact him.

This is the brilliance of the no contact regulation. It not only gives your ex time to miss you, but also gives YOU time to get your mind on straight. Obviously, the majority of women who attempt no contact and fail do so because they lack the patience and (confidence in their own abilities) required to get their ex to pursue.

Avoid doing the following during the no contact period:

-Spending the day resting due to how one feels.

Staying in and avoiding the outdoors.

-Getting drunk on yourself.

-Informing the entire universe of your breakup.

-Making monumental life choices.

Frequent work absences.

Consider the following: he will likely text or call during this no contact period. It is essential that you ignore him.

-You may learn from mutual friends that he has been calling you derogatory names, or you may get the impression that he cannot abide you and wants nothing to do with you. Don't be concerned, he is merely emotional and lashing out. After thirty days, he will inevitably alter his tune.

Being in contact with your ex is the opposite of being out of contact. It is the time during which you are permitted to communicate with your ex-boyfriend.

As difficult as patience was with no contact, being in communication with your ex can be even more challenging, assuming you've successfully completed the 30-day no contact period and are now in contact with your ex.

When texting anyone (not just your ex) to make them chase you, quality block texting is likely the single most essential tactic to employ. Here's an example of quality blocking: a television program is intended to end on a cliffhanger so that viewers will return the following week. Now, the same principle applies to your texting conversations with individuals you're interested in, just as it does to television episodes. I'll explain why in a moment.

But that's not all. After pausing the conversation with a cliffhanger for three to five hours, text him again and repeat the process until you have him captivated. Do you see what is occurring? You are dividing the texts into segments of quality time over which you have complete control. I determine when the text messages begin and end. However, there are numerous irregularities associated with that. The QBT method necessitates a great deal of logical reasoning. In order to determine when to end a conversation with your ex, you must be logical, which can be challenging if you have already established a solid relationship. There is a certain level of solace in "getting responses," and it can be extremely difficult to know when to end a conversation when emotions are involved.

Reasons He Might Have Dumped You

Getting rejected stinks. I understand how you feel, but you have nothing to worry about because I will guide you through what you need to do and realize to get your partner back, regardless of the reason and the cost. Do not assume that the explanation your ex-partner gave you for breaking up with you is the actual reason. It may sound harsh, but you will need to be entirely honest and receptive as I describe the potential causes below, and you will need to give them careful consideration.

Here are several of the most prevalent causes of breakups:

Your spouse was no longer attracted to you:

It may be painful to acknowledge, but this is a legitimate REAL reason why many men terminate relationships with their girlfriends. This is a common complaint among men who are in a relationship with a woman who became a little too secure around them and relaxed during the relationship. Believe me when I say that your physical appearance is much simpler to enhance than your personality, so don't let this discourage you. It simply means you need to exert a little more effort on occasion.

Your ex-partner grew weary of you:

This is another valid reason to end a relationship. Sadly, it speaks more about him and his bad attitude or lack of effort (unless you had a dead personality, which is extremely improbable) than it does about anything you did. But fortunately, being monotonous can often be easily remedied!

The sexual and emotional requirements of your boyfriends were not met by you:

Quite frequently, this can occur without your knowledge. Men are not the greatest at expressing themselves, particularly when delivering bad news. The last thing they want to do is cause you pain or embarrassment, so they will simply break up with you and give you another vague reason. Fortunately, this can also be rectified!

Your ex is unsure of what he desires:

In this instance, the cliche "it's not you, it's me" holds true. This one can be a little more difficult to recover from, but believe me, it is possible if you approach the situation intelligently.

He may have committed adultery and desired to be with that person:

When it comes to cheating, there is only one thing you need to comprehend. Men and women deceive for vastly distinct motives.

Because they are eager, men cheat. Because their emotional requirements were not being met, women cheat.

Once they are settled with their new spouse, exes frequently recognize the things they neglected about you but may have taken for granted.

As a general rule, it is preferable to have a legitimate reason for wanting to reunite with a former partner. However, the following factors are NOT acceptable.

-Declaring that you cannot survive without him.

-He is your complete existence.

-You will never find someone as capable as he.

-You are not content being alone.

-Next time will be different.

Again, these are insufficient grounds for reconciliation. If you are uttering any of these things, you can get along just fine without this individual.

Here are some acceptable explanations.

The decision to end the relationship was a half-hearted one.

-You had a major argument that led to your separation.

-You were essentially content the entire time you were together.

-You both desire the same things in a shared existence.

Recognizing Where Your Relationship Went Wrong

No split is ever simple. When a once-healthy and productive relationship deteriorates, the pain and bitterness emanating from either partner has a way of seeping into your system, causing you to feel depressed and possibly remorseful. This is especially true when, after a thorough evaluation of the relationship, you realize that your ex-girlfriend still means everything to you and that losing her would be the worst thing that could happen to you. Therefore, you find yourself pondering if it is still possible to regain her former love and affection.

Getting your ex-girlfriend back into your life is thankfully not unattainable. In truth, as you will discover after reading the remainder of this book, there are a few strategies and techniques you can employ to win back the love and affection she once had for you (and possibly still has). The key is to be certain of your feelings and assertive enough to take matters into your own hands, with the end objective of regaining her in your life.

determining the underlying cause

However, you must first determine the primary reason why you and your ex broke up. Understanding the reason for your breakup is essential for developing a plan to gain her back. A misguided approach may not yield positive results, so you must have a thorough comprehension of which aspect of your relationship requires attention. Otherwise, you run the risk of engaging in a fruitless endeavor.

Accepting the cause of your relationship's failure has a number of benefits, one of which is that it helps you understand yourself better. By recognizing your own character flaws or weaknesses, you become more aware of the aspects of yourself that you need to concentrate on and alter for the best. At the same time, this information provides you with the motivation to pursue her again, secure in the knowledge that you have carefully considered the repercussions of your actions and are now ready to start over.

Resolving issues

Until all issues pertaining to your relationship have been resolved, refrain from engaging in any activity that involves it. For instance, if you are at a loss as to what caused the relationship to disintegrate and fail, you may wish to conduct a form of self-examination.

Did you lavish so much affection and attention on your partner that she began to feel suffocated? Or perhaps the reverse was true. Did you give your companion so little time and consideration that she felt insignificant and uncared for? Different priorities or the presence of a third party may have contributed to your relationship's deterioration. Or did your relationship dissolve due to tedium and a lack of passion? Note that regardless of the cause, you should endeavor to learn from it as you move forward with your plan.

In conclusion, you have every right to pursue your ex-girlfriend back into your life in the hopes of rekindling your former romantic relationship. To avoid additional suffering and disappointment, you must, however, support this desire with the appropriate knowledge and strategies. You must possess a similar sense of timing to see your plan through to its conclusion. Importantly, all of your efforts must stem from a sincere desire to make amends for your flaws and develop in a relationship that brings out the best in you and your partner.

Day 1 – Clear Your Mind The Reasons Men Leave a Relationship

Frequent break-ups occur between couples. Different factors motivate men and women to end relationships. It can be difficult to decipher the psyche of the opposite sex, but you can attempt to comprehend their motivation.

Men are sensitive to your emotions. Or perhaps they simply do not want to hear your response to the truth. Some males have no idea why they want out of the relationship; they simply do.

Men will leave a relationship when it no longer meets their needs, regardless of the circumstances. Men desire admiration for who they are. They want to be treated with respect and to feel your interest.

When a relationship becomes stagnant, men may look for another woman who demonstrates the same level of freshness and interest as you once did. You can refer to it as manhood or ego, but it is simply how males are. Let him feel this admiration, or he will receive it from another source.

Men do not quit because they have found a more attractive or thinner partner. They leave to once again feel respected, revered, and desired. They do not want to be constantly nagged. The act of nagging conveys to him that you are dissatisfied with who he is and what he has to offer, and this causes him to withdraw from the relationship.

This does not mean you can never express your true emotions, but you must balance them with an expression of love and admiration that will fuel the flame of your relationship. To keep your partner happy, you need not sacrifice your self-respect and cater to his every whim.

Reasons for Separation

Relationship breakups are frequently extremely agonizing because nobody begins a relationship with the intention of having it end badly. However, relationship breakdowns rarely occur without cause. As with all things in the universe, everything occurs for a purpose.

Every day, more relationships disintegrate, and the list of potential causes seems infinite. However, the majority of the leading causes of death are relatively basic, such as misunderstanding. This is extremely hurtful if you have shown your companion the utmost love, causing you to hope that everything will be resolved between you two as soon as possible.

Now, what are the most common causes of couple breakups? Here are some common explanations:

• Dishonesty and infidelity – Lying and adultery are never beneficial to a relationship. Who desires to be in a relationship with a liar and a cheater?

• Dominant partner and constant pestering – It's aggravating to hear your partner ask you about irrelevant matters. This is likely to result in an argument.

• "Not-so-sweet" nature – Some individuals are simply not demonstrative about their emotions for their partners. This could be misconstrued as a lack of concern.

- Controlling – Hounding your companion will give them the impression that they are your "property." They may wish to 'breakaway' from you if they feel they are losing their independence.

- Mistrust – When you have trust in your companion, you feel secure and loved because you know he or she is devoted and faithful. What's the purpose of being in a relationship if you no longer trust your partner?

- Contradictory differences – If your partner desires children and you do not, this could pose a problem.

- Loss of love – One or both of you appear to have lost the 'spark' that once existed in the relationship.

- Boredom – Any relationship loses its appeal when it becomes predictable.

When it comes to relationships, spontaneity is essential.

• Frequent conflicts – Arguments and fights cause a great deal of stress, leaving no space for love. Cute, petty disputes may add spice to a relationship, but protracted arguments do not.

• Independence – You or your companion may not require support or assistance from anyone, making it difficult to maintain a relationship.

• maltreatment – This may include mental or physical maltreatment, and reconciliation may be impossible.

• Physical Incompatibility – You may disagree on what is physically desirable, such as you prefer long hair and he prefers short hair.

• Distance – Some individuals are simply not enamored of long-distance relationships. Therefore, when one of them transfers to a distant location, the relationship cannot continue.

- Irritability – One or both of you may find the other or one of the other's habits irritating.

Regardless of the reason, there is always some level of involvement, even if it is passive. Similarly, it takes two to tango, and it requires two to have a relationship. When the reason for the breakup is readily controllable, you may sometimes refuse to acknowledge it. However, understanding the reason for the breakup will bring you one step closer to reuniting with your ex, provided you do not repeat the same error.

Pointing Fingers

You do not have to be the dumped party to initiate a reconciliation with your former. Your ex may have moved on by the time you realize you made a blunder, if you are the one who dumped them.

Regardless of who was at fault, you must be willing to assume responsibility for your share of errors. To have a successful relationship, you must cease pointing fingers at each other. However, before you can do so, you must completely accept yourself. Do some introspection.

Post Break Up Drama

Following a breakup, you will experience a variety of emotions. You may currently feel depressed, confused, and wounded, but a breakup does not necessarily indicate that the relationship has ended.

It's common to experience loneliness. This is not necessarily a negative sign, as it indicates that you care about your ex and are open to finding methods to bring him or her back into your life.

However, you must develop the self-assurance that will prevent you from engaging in detrimental behavior, which can make matters worse for you and your partner. If you manage the situation with confidence, you will almost certainly have an easier time regaining your partner.

Obviously, it will take some time for you to regain your cheerful disposition after a breakup, but if you're optimistic and self-assured, it will do wonders for your chances of reuniting with your former.

One of the most common ways that individuals cope with suffering is by binge eating or binge drinking. These are both destructive behaviors that can damage your body and your ability to think logically. This type of behavior can cause you to lose concentration and demolish any chance of reconciliation.

Avoid destructive behaviors when attempting to contend with the stress of a breakup. You must cultivate a healthy lifestyle, which can aid in the recovery process following a breakup or separation and increase your possibilities of reuniting with your ex.

Why Would You Like to Reunite?

You believe you want your ex-lover to return. Obviously, it won't work if everything remains the same as before the breakup. Before attempting reconciliation, you must take time for yourself to recover and regain your sense of self.

After the end of your recuperation period, if you still want to be with your ex, you should consider why. There are many causes besides true love for which one may act. Consider whether you want to rekindle an old relationship for the following motives:

- Your ex is with a new partner, and your ego is wounded – You cannot accept the fact that your ex-partner hooked up with another person so shortly after your breakup.

- You're beating yourself up over the breakup – You only want to reconcile with your ex because your mind is urging you to do so in order to regain control.

- You are on the receiving end of a breakup, and your ego is once again wounded – You want your ex-partner back to satisfy your ego. You are no longer passionately in love with your ex-partner, but you want to know how to woo them back.

• You never fully let go of the issues that led to the end of the relationship, or you never saw the conclusion as a positive – You believe that your ex is the only person who will want you and make you happy because you have not reestablished your trust in other potential companions.

• You want your ex to experience the same pain and anguish that you did – Essentially, the only reason you want your ex back is so that you can reject them. Allow him to experience his own remedy.

These motives are all governed by the ego. Sure, you've been wounded, we've all been there. And if you are sincere with yourself, you have also been on the receiving end. Such is reality. There is always a reason why one or both parties in a relationship fail to succeed.

Reuniting with an ex can be successful, but often both parties need time to regain their footing. The majority of the time, you return to the past because you fear the future. Remember that you cannot live in the past or in anticipation of the future. You must reside in the present.

Whether It's A No Or A Yes

Every flow includes a trough. A wave cannot move forward until it has first moved backwards.

Therefore, the next stage in getting your ex back entails trying to completely forget about him.

Avoid all contact with him. Put yourself in the spotlight. Observe yourself.

Consider: What do I require? What do I feel like doing tonight? What do I think of this film or television program?

Examine the rationale for this action.

A relationship, especially one that is deteriorating, can resemble a greenhouse. Partners can lose perspective amidst the pressures of attempting to maintain the relationship, juggling employment, and raising children. Adults need space and a sense of self to be healthy.

But when in a relationship, it can be alluring to define yourself as 'we' rather than 'I'. "We like going to the gym." "We watch The Killing in the evenings." We believe that the government's policies are erroneous. Occasionally, your emotions and viewpoints can be incorporated by the partnership.

In the anxiety to please the other person and be the partner they desire, it is simple to neglect what you truly believe and feel. When a relationship is in its final stages and you perceive that things aren't working out, it can be tempting to suppress your thoughts and emotions even more. To do everything necessary to retain his affection.

And thus begins a vicious cycle. The more one denies his or her own needs and emotions, the more one loses his or her identity. And you become increasingly incapable of being the independent, contented partner your soulmate requires.

Partners can become so engrossed in each other that, almost unwittingly, they neglect or lose sight of things or activities that were significant to them. Occasionally, they view this sacrifice as necessary for the sake of the relationship — a gesture that should strengthen their connection.

Perhaps long walks were an integral part of your existence for many years. Something that restored your emotional equilibrium and made you feel better.

But your partner doesn't like extended walks. He'd rather watch football in the afternoons. He claims it has great significance when viewed alongside him.

You believe that giving up your walks is not a significant sacrifice. Surely, the best course of action is to spend time with my companion, even if we only watch football together.

However, giving up the items you adore is difficult.

The items you cherish define who you are. They allow you to be a whole, self-sufficient person who is fascinating, lovable, and most importantly, complete in yourself.

No one desires a partner who disregards their own needs. Let's be straightforward here. This individual will have nothing to say. This individual is tedious, predictable, and dependent. They will not challenge their companion by bringing new experiences into the relationship or helping them to develop.

A partner who disregards their own requirements is most likely to be taken for granted.

Ask yourself: Have I lost contact with the things that gave me a sense of identity throughout this relationship? Am I no longer in contact with myself?

Is this a factor in why I feel so disoriented without my ex? Have I begun to rely on him for my sense of self?

Can I alter this and become a complete individual again? So that even if I were to never see him again, I would still feel content?

These inquiries may cause you to feel uneasy or even guilty. Particularly women are taught that love equals sacrifice. That if you truly adore someone, you will sacrifice things for them, such as your hobbies and ambitions. We are aware that this is false and unjust, but these emotions remain potent.

You may believe that asking, "Can I become the type of person who could be happy on her own?" is a betrayal of your ex. A declaration that you do not need or want him. This is not the case in any way. If you are fulfilled in yourself, you can love others more powerfully and effectively.

Now is the time for Start reconnecting with the things you adore in Activity 2.

For some, this immediately poses a problem. "I cannot recall what I enjoy doing!" The demands of home, family, and work have become overwhelming. Sometimes it can be difficult to recall the last time you did something for yourself.

Therefore, engage in an ideation session and compose a list of activities you once enjoyed.

Review your previous journals.

Rewatch old films and television programs you once enjoyed.

Reread beloved works.

Meet up with former acquaintances.

Thus, you will begin to recall the things you once enjoyed. You will begin reconnecting with the individual you once were.

However, do not engage in frenetic activity. Some friends will advise you to keep very occupied. They believe that it will help you feel better and forget the agony of the breakup. This is excellent short-term advice if the relationship has ended but you're trying to win your ex back permanently.

Instead of promptly filling your schedule, create space in your life for yourself. Provide yourself with opportunities to consider your long-term goals. Your aims, aspirations, and objectives. Your character and priorities.

When are you most content?

Which activities do you enjoy the most?

What type of companion can best assist you in pursuing your goals?

Is your ex he or she?

These are significant concerns. Ten, five, or two years ago, you may have believed a certain answer to be correct. Make every effort to consider these questions from beginning.

When you believe you have found answers to these queries, it is time to get to work. Spend a minimum of one month immersed in your interests and activities.

There is no correct action or set of actions at this time. It depends greatly on your personality and your interests.

Be vigilant. Many individuals will hurry into a frenzy of self-improvement. They make hundreds of resolutions - to lose weight, begin exercising, and read more - and it can be beneficial to feel like you have objectives at this point.

However, resolutions are difficult to maintain at the best of times, let alone when you are in the midst of a painful breakup. If you make too many unrealistic resolutions, you will feel miserable, guilty, and hateful of yourself when you violate them.

Make one or no more than two. You could commit to routinely swimming with a friend. Or by taking treks. Keep it compact, entertaining, and satisfying.

Other advice:

Alternate between physical and mental activity.

Rekindle your appreciation for beauty. Bring back color and shape into your existence. Poetry, art, and nature are all effective methods for this.

Make something. Creating something, whether it's a delicious meal, a stitched purse, or an origami swan, will boost your confidence and sense of self-worth.

As you engage in self-care, you will feel enriched and rewarded. You will find yourself chuckling more, anticipating the next day, and interacting with others in a joyful and animated manner. This procedure will transform you back into the person your ex fell in love with initially. Within the confines of an intense relationship, adjustments will be made to your characteristics that have become less endearing.

Moreover, this process may provide you with clarity.

There is no correct emotion. And it is possible that you will find happiness in a manner that you did not while you were with your ex.

For some women, this is the final stage in the procedure. Once they have reconnected with themselves, they realize they no longer require their former. He may have held you back or caused you unhappiness in ways you were unaware of.

Some women realize that they can live fuller, more satisfying lives on their own or with another person.

If this describes you, congratulations on your lucid reasoning and courage. And best wishes for your new life's path.

Even though you may feel happier and tranquil after a month, you may still be convinced that your ex is the one for you. And you may feel more prepared than ever to begin a lifelong relationship with him. Consequently, it is time for the next phase...

How To Get Over Your Obsessions...And Get Over Your Ex

I have excellent news to share.

Though it may seem impossible, it is possible to overcome your ex and all the emotional baggage a divorce may cause.

You can begin to take command of your life (and your heartbreak) once you've identified the signs that are holding you back, which I believe you've done.

This can be accomplished by learning how to speak about where you are, expanding your concept of self, and redefining the things that make you truly come alive – joyful, content, and at ease with the world.

Before we get into how to get over your ex, you may want to read this true tale about a woman (I'll call her Jane) who reclaimed her power after a devastating breakup.

Michael and I ended our relationship a few weeks before he began medical school.

Our relationship was like a tornado. Before he moved from Connecticut to Pennsylvania and into my one-bedroom apartment, we had only been dating for two weeks.

A few months later, we were engaged in wedding preparations. We deliberated over the selection of wedding favors and visited jewelers to try on engagement rings.

I was ecstatic, overjoyed, and, of course, certain he was "the one."

Then, not too long after that, we were suddenly on the rocks. Even in the shortest phone conversations, an argument broke out. Weekend excursions resulted in shouting and sobbing.

Exactly nine months after the start of our relationship, I found myself sitting in my parked car after work, dialing his number in a moment of confusion and terror. "I told him I'm not getting what I want."In the night that followed my separation, I had this dramatic push-pull experience that nearly everyone goes through.

One moment I was on top of the world and confident in my decision, the next I was convinced that my ex would return and certain that I had made the correct choice. And abruptly heartbroken, numb, and terrified.

Brain Boutwell, an evolutionary psychologist at St. Louis University, provided me with scientific explanations for my melancholy.

He stated that falling in love and cocaine addiction share the same neural circuitry.

"Falling in love is comparable to an addictive process. You have a need to be with the individual you care about in order to satisfy that craving."

Thus, according to Boutwell, your separation was a cocaine withdrawal.

Oh, it's just heartbreak; it's not that big of a problem, after all. Unlike breakups, which can be a risk factor for depression and, of course, can be emotionally devastating, depression is not a clinical condition to be taken lightly. Separations can be hazardous to one's wellbeing."

After the separation, I felt physically ill, emotionally drained, and physically exhausted.

At one of these particularly low points, I became enraged with myself, my ex, and the ridiculous situation as a whole.

How dare he not work harder to maintain this relationship?

How dare something so magnificent and promising come to an end?

How dare I, as an outspoken feminist who constantly promotes women's independence, power, pride, and resilience, betray women by acting as if my life was over due to something as trivial as a breakup?

What actually transpired?

I had lost a companion, a man, and a friend, but I had not lost myself.

As a result, I set out on a mission to reclaim myself, turning this separation into an opportunity for self-discovery and revitalization rather than an excuse to feel sorry for myself.

I attempted everything, from blocking my ex on every conceivable social media platform to reconnecting with old friends.

An incredible story isn't it?

As you embark on the journey to reclaim your freedom and happiness, I hope that Jane's story will inspire you to make the necessary adjustments.

All of this will become clearer as you proceed to the next chapter and review the steps to get over your ex for good.

Therefore, let's not halt here!

Spend some time in thought

Breakups stink.

And our brains are essentially hardwired to resist it and grieve the loss of a relationship.

REFLECTION is one of the most potent healing weapons in your arsenal, but it requires a bit of practice.

Looking back on your failed relationships can reveal a wealth of insights that enable you to make better decisions in the future. Moreover, it results in more fulfilling and productive interpersonal relationships.

This requires honesty on your part and the realization that improvement is always accompanied by a degree of discomfort.

"Don't tuck your ex away in a far-off corner, intent on returning another day. Instead of attempting to cover or bury the emotions you feel after a breakup, you embrace them and the thoughts (both positive and negative) that you have about your former partner or spouse.

Studies have shown that contemplating a separation – using the correct terminology – is an excellent way to unravel the mysteries and discover the silver lining in any breakup.

When you reflect thoughtfully on what went wrong and what went well, it becomes simpler to accept things as they are and to move on in a more efficient and complete manner.

I urge you to consider what led to the separation and why it occurred. Remember that things went awry and the relationship ended as a result. Accepting how the situation transpired is essential for moving on.

You presumably realized by now that things were not going well prior to the breakup, so it was inevitable that the relationship would end.

Recognize that you are both better off now that the relationship is over.

Therefore, if you're still fixated on your ex because you can't stop avoiding the notion, you should slow down. You must confront the past in order to progress beyond it.

You must completely accept your emotions.

Understanding breakups can profoundly affect our emotions. Moreover, how we perceive our other relationships and the universe.

If you're not careful, the agony of an unresolved heartbreak can turn into a life-altering mess that undermines your joy, happiness, and success.

According to relationship expert and clinical psychologist Dr. Carmen Harra, the key to overcoming the difficulty and hardship of a significant heartbreak is dealing with our emotions. To recover from a divorce and prevent it from happening again in the future, you must control your emotions. Obsession causes one to become mired in the past. But if you can think logically and recognize the need to progress forward, you will be able to control your emotions."

You cannot possibly move forward unless you process the complex emotions triggered by a serious breach of trust, but doing so requires radical self-acceptance and considerable bravery.

Take some time to process your sorrow, anger, hatred, shock, and grief in response to what has occurred. Permit your emotions to flow freely in the present and let them come to you as they are, with no need to suppress or alter them.

Moreover, mind journaling practices are an excellent method to connect with your emotions in a safe and accepting environment.

You may wish to rest in a quiet area and remain grounded in the present as you access the emotions that are causing you the most turmoil in your life.

Be mindful when making observations, and don't be hesitant to describe how you're feeling or what's causing your emotions to fluctuate.

You get?

The blame game will not assist you; give it up!

As humans, the blame game is one of our preferred coping mechanisms, but it is also one of the most self-defeating and destructive behaviors, as well as one that undermines our relationships.

When things don't go as planned, we love to blame ourselves (and everyone else) in order to divert our attention away from the actual issues and the necessary changes.

"We frequently project our negative feelings and emotions onto others in order to feel better about ourselves, and we even internalize the negative for others as a form of "self-sacrifice"

We are adept at playing the blame game, but it is a toxic pattern to fall into when experiencing grief.

Sometimes, recognize that there is no one to accuse and that things simply occur. However, you must embrace that, as well as the fact that sometimes our plans don't work out as we had hoped.

You must stop blaming yourself for whatever went wrong and recognize that you deserve compassion, honesty, and love as much as anyone else in the universe.

Unresolved remorse generates resentment and hostility. So, let go of your need to place sole responsibility on your shoulders and take charge of your feelings.

Plan your recovery strategy

To overcome your grief and ex, you must have a general plan (or blueprint) of where you're going and what we must do to restore your happiness.

Instead of merely accepting the default of your heartbreak, design the existence you desire. And the best way to accomplish this is to spend some time introspecting and reconnecting with that once-trusting, once-loving self.

Take the time to sit down and create a recovery plan that works for you and your future objectives – without any pressure or whatsoever.

Understand that the end of a relationship reveals something about both parties.

Instead of dwelling on the act itself, focus on how it has made you feel.

"Focus on your emotions and the resources you need to manage the situation. You can either forget or forgive, or you can put some distance between yourself and the situation and take some time to contemplate what you need and where you need to go."

Unhealthy is holding on to negative emotions and fumbling around in the dark.

Reach out to a trusted family member or friend, a mentor, a coach, or a counselor for their perspective on the situation if you are unsure of how to proceed.

Again, mindful journaling can be extremely helpful in identifying the actions you must take to make the best of a situation.

Consider the following advice from a friend genuinely invested in your success. "Only you can define your own healing,"

No strain!

Just take the necessary time to formulate a plan that you can adhere to.

Pardon yourself

Most self-help books and articles emphasize the importance of forgiving those who have wronged us, but they frequently overlook the significance of forgiving ourselves.

I believe that experiencing a relationship collapse not only results in a loss of trust in others, but also in a loss of self-trust.

When we experience these types of breakups, we often interpret them as a reflection of who we are, leading to self-doubt that is both self-defeating and corrosive.

Self-forgiveness does not imply accepting the pitfalls you slipped into or the errors you made.

No!

It merely entails detaching yourself from the bitterness, anguish, and rage that are buried deep within you, eating away at who you are and the future you have planned for yourself.

"The only true forgiveness you need to seek in the flaming wreckage of betrayal is your own."

As humans, we are susceptible to blunders and errors. No one is flawless, and no one ever makes all the correct decisions at all times.

Consider this a learning curve and an opportunity, and have enough compassion for yourself to allow for setbacks along the way.

Having animosity hinders your advancement. Forgive yourself and give yourself the power to make the necessary changes to your life and relationships.

Take your leisure

Time and space is a formidable force. And this is especially accurate regarding relationship dissolution.

When we give ourselves time and a certain measure of physical or emotional distance from our former partners, we also give ourselves the gift of perspective.

This then enables us to see things as they are and rehabilitate.

If you still find yourself fixated on an ex, try taking a step back and giving yourself space to grieve, weep, and move on.

Providing yourself with space and distance can take any form necessary. While this may involve isolating yourself from certain social circles for a period of time, it may also involve taking a solo trip to an exotic location, deleting your ex's social media accounts, and blocking their number as well as the numbers of anyone who might attempt to interfere.

If you are genuinely struggling after a significant breakup, you must give yourself space to breathe.

Limit interruptions regardless of how far away you are, and ensure that you cannot be interrupted by Christmas spirits.

Numerous studies demonstrate that time is an effective remedy. And when combined with distance, it can significantly enhance your emotional attachment.

The greater the distance between you and the person you can't stop thinking about, the quicker you can emotionally recuperate.

However, it cannot be done quickly. Healing cannot be expedited or hastened. Obviously, your suffering will not vanish overnight. It can only improve over time.

Date yourself

Allow yourself the opportunity to appreciate yourself.

This is one of the most effective methods to move on from an ex who refuses to leave your memories alone.

I've observed that when we enter into relationships, we tend to lose perspective of the things that bring us genuine joy and happiness, and in the process, we lose ourselves.

However, by dating yourself, you can learn how to fall in love with yourself again and also acquire a deeper understanding of all the beautiful and unique characteristics that make you, you. Instead of focusing on someone who no longer wants to celebrate you, you can learn to celebrate yourself, thereby empowering your own rehabilitation.

Focus on yourself and take a step back from socializing. Treat yourself as you would expect or desire your significant other to treat you.

Buy yourself flowers, greeting cards, and small treats that make you feel happy, and dine at upscale restaurants.

Learn how to physically and emotionally treat yourself the way you would want a partner to treat you.

Start by being there for yourself (in word and deed) and altering your inner dialogue.

Transform the voice of your inner critic into the voice of your inner admirer, and treat yourself as you would a partner.

You're aware of what?

Not only will you begin to notice significant changes in the way you view yourself, but also in your perspective on the relationship. When you prioritize self-love, you place a higher value on your emotions and time.

You will realize that your heart is a valuable asset that is not worth giving to the lowest bidder (i.e., your ex or any unserious man) as opposed to giving yourself away to people who don't value and want you.

The key, however, is to first be the type of lover you desire, and you will attract the type of lover you desire.

THE GOLDEN RULE: DO NOT FOLLOW OTHERS

As previously stated, a breakup can induce extreme emotions, leading to inappropriate behavior. In other words, when you are distraught about a breakup, you are not yourself. The most common error people make is allowing their dread to guide them so much that they become instantaneous stalkers. You do not want your ex to view you as an uncontrollable stalker who is harassing him/her with menacing messages or untimely declarations of love. If this is a no-no when meeting someone for the first time, it should be the golden rule for those who want their ex-lover back.

Here are some guidelines to follow that will make you a winner rather than a "maniac."

-Be sensible: First, if you want to get far in your quest to get your former back, you must always be reasonable, which means you must return to your senses whenever you feel discouraged or unable to continue. Despite the fact that it is entirely possible for you to be afraid, given that your ex could have moved on or could reject you in the future.

The following is a list of things you should and should not do:

-Don't call him/her immediately after the separation or before you've devised a plan to win them back. Because you must be composed enough to devise a plan that will allow you to confront your ex.

Imagine that you and your ex-partner broke up for very significant reasons, such as lack of trust or him (or her) keeping a secret from you. How do you think he/she will view you if you return to him/her after every breakup because you can't bear being without him/her, despite the fact that you had every reason to dump him/her? You surely don't want him or her to perceive you as weak or emotionally unstable.

-Do not express your emotions to close acquaintances in the hope that they will assist you in reuniting. Do not cry to your common acquaintances. Numerous individuals would because they require reassurance. You are mistaken for the simple reason that you do not know who they support or who they consider a close friend, and it is always preferable to send a message to a person yourself as opposed to relying on others to do so. Instead, you should make a fleeting reference to the breakup and then move on to another topic. Thus, you will appear more confident and composed.

-Instead of isolating yourself, do something (be active). The longer you are alone, the greater the temptation to do something foolish, such as crying and calling your ex to implore him/her to take you back. You may view it as a simple solution, but the reality is that your ex will perceive you as a distressed person who will be attached to him or her. Too many emotions are never desirable. What should matter is having a firm plan to rebuild your relationship with your ex. Instead, go to the movies, pay a friend a visit, work out, and unwind during the limited time you will have to strategize and win back your ex.

-Do prioritize yourself. Consider your future desires in terms of relationships. Spend some time answering the following queries: What do I hope to accomplish in the relationship? What am I looking for in a partner? How much energy and positivity can I invest in this relationship for it to succeed?

This should be the beginning of a voyage to win back your ex. The relevant keywords are "do not panic and maintain composure."

-The influence of time: Time is viewed as an abstract concept, but when utilized effectively, one can accomplish a great deal. In the Western world, time equates money, so all tasks must be completed quickly. When it comes to emotions, time becomes a very delicate concept. You do not know how your ex feels, what he/she does currently, or what he/she intends to do in the future, so you must plan your new seduction strategy carefully.

Therefore, take your time. In actuality, you will need seven days. Give yourself seven days to formulate a plan and muster the strength to reclaim your ex.

Breakups can be brutal, untimely, and difficult to explain, particularly for the discarded party. You may find yourself in a situation where you see an unexpected visage of your partner. Since we are discussing emotions, however, everyone has their own reasons for loving, and since true love is superior to authoritarianism, materialism, and stupidity, everyone has a chance at it. This means that you are justified in giving your ex a second opportunity or in seeking a second chance (depending on the circumstance).

In order to improve your communication skills with your ex once you're back together, planning, regaining your composure, and considering what you'd like to see altered are therefore essential. Here is a list of suggestions for organizing your week before contacting your ex:

-Day 1 (the day you realized you desired your ex back): Consider this idea throughout the day. Take some time to consider the positive aspects of your relationship, as a means of weighing the relationship's pros and cons. This will help you determine what you may receive if you reconcile with your ex. You may have ended your relationship a year or a week ago, but there is a reason you still have sentiments for that person. In this case, time will help you gain a better perspective and perhaps begin your relationship anew with a new and more mature attitude.

-Day 2: After weighing the pros and cons of your lost relationship on day 1, begin strategizing on day 2 (there are only six days left). Here is where you must consider what you will say and what you believe will have the most impact (this is crucial, as you may only have one opportunity). You could have separated a year ago or just days ago, but you still need a plan. Consider what you would say the first time you see your ex again on day 2. For example, instead of beginning with "I felt compelled to tell you something," begin with "How are you?" "It has been a while" Remember to be intelligent in your conversation, and to say something that will put everyone at ease and make them smile. Prepare yourself for it. Create a list of five introductory phrases such as "how are you?" and "what have you been doing all this time?" and practice them. Because the purpose of such introductory phrases is to encourage everyone to unwind and open up, be sure to use a casual tone.

Day 3: Nourish yourself with pleasant memories. It is a form of motivational technique designed to remind you why you are undertaking all of this. It is possible that you feel your ex is what is missing from your life at the moment, that you feel stupid for letting such a special person go, or that you feel the only thing separating the two of you is your ego, and you want to make amends to him/her before someone else does. Consider the times you chuckled together, as well as your complicity with that individual. Create an inventory of the benefits the relationship brought to your life at the end of the day, and consider the type of person you were. Consider the following: Were you happier? What made you pleased about this individual? This is significant because these details may be the ties that bind the two of you, and if you bring them up with your ex, he or she will realize how special the relationship is.

-Day 4: On day 4, consider your ex's preferences. Is he or she a romantic? Will he or she be delighted by a hotel stay for the two of you? Remember that you are reconquering someone, so you must remind him or her how special he or she is; you may even need to flatter your ex (but not excessively). Overall, you must demonstrate that, due to your spontaneity and (wonderful) ability to astonish others, you are worth taking back.

Consider what you must do to "wow" this person after your first engagement, and consider the following: Sending him/her flowers and making a public declaration of affection on Facebook. Go on a date at a luxurious hotel outside the city, think of something original but extravagant, and make your ex feel as special as you've never made them feel before. Remember that you must reignite the flame, and your ex must fall in love with you again to the extent that he or she will brag about you for weeks. Choose one or a combination of two or three items that you believe your ex will enjoy by the end of the day.

-Day 5: On day 5, you must focus on believing that you will be successful in reuniting with your former. What would be the point of going through all of this if you did not believe you will be successful in regaining him/her? You should also be aware that when attempting to persuade someone (who may have differing opinions, wish to move on, etc.), anything can happen because, well, people change. You may have known your ex for some time, but his goals may have changed (depending on the length of your separation). So, be positive, think positively, and tell yourself, for example, "I will succeed" instead of "I hope everything goes well." You will find that when the time comes, you will know exactly what to say because your primary objective is to get your ex back regardless of the circumstances. Do not allow doubt to control you; instead, repeat these affirmative statements over and over.

-Day Six: On day six, consider where you should meet with your ex and how you will convince him or her to do so. Consider a discreet location where you can easily make an impression. The feedback you receive could be positive or negative (you never know), but the impact of what you have to say and the environment you choose will make such a nice combination that the person with negative feedback might think twice about that moment later on that day and wonder, "Huh, it felt quite nice out there; what if he/she had a point?" Believe us when we say that no one can resist a pleasant setting for a romantic conversation.

Here is a hint on which sets to choose depending on whether you are interacting with a male or a woman:

If your ex was female: Women prefer tranquil environments with warm hues, whether they are natural or artificial. Consider a safe, clean, and beautiful public park with trees and enough flowers, or a nice, cozy restaurant (not a fast food joint), surprise her, and capture that smile that will make her blush and feel comfortable around you once more.

-If your ex is a male, avoid meeting him in a distracting environment. Do not take him to see his beloved movie or a sporting event. He will be happy to be there, but after the adrenaline rush is gone, he will come back to reality and no matter what he would have said while being at the movies or watching the game, will not matter anymore. Consider a site where he will be able to concentrate on you two. Think of something simple, like a fast food restaurant (where the mood is joyous and nobody cares about how you look like but is just there to have a quick bite).

Overall, on day 6, you will have to base your decisions on the specifics if you are dealing with a woman, and on capturing the individual's attention if you are dealing with a male.

-Day 7: Day 7, is an important day because this is the day when you will call your ex to tell him/her that you would like to meet with him/her.

Here are the guidelines to follow on day 7:

-First, contact your ex in the morning around noon, if your seventh day falls on a Monday to Friday. Noon is perfect because it¡¦s normally the time around which most people take their lunch break, or eat lunch. Lunch breaks normally last 30 minutes (minimum), and that's enough time to speak with your ex. If it's a weekend day, call at 10 AM, people sleep longer, and also this will be a nice surprise for your ex as your voice will be the first thing he/she hears.

-Then, start your conversation by asking how she/he is doing. After that, ask if he/she has some free time during the week or the weekend (don't set it too early or too late). If the person can't make up his/her mind; propose a day. If he/she comes up with a day that is too far (like 8 or 9 days after your call), ask if it can be done sooner and propose a preferred date. This will allow you to "work on your ex" faster and not lose your focus on the essential which is to stay positive, all the time.

-End up by making sure you "touch your ex's sensitivity" by saying something like "I couldn't spend another week without meeting you, I hope to see you on X day" then you say goodbye and hang up. Your last sentence (like the one mentioned above should be said with a serious and warm tone. You will plunge your ex immediately into the past when your feelings towards one another were strong and you felt like you couldn't leave without one another. This is the part where your ex will definitely come and meet you to hear what you have to say.

Now, that you know what you need to do, let's move on to the next phase.

WHEN AN EXCELLENT RELATIONSHIP FAILS

There is a cause for the breakdown of relationships. It will never be fair as long as there is no longer love and pleasure. Something is incorrect. It could include recurring conflicts and arguments, broken promises, incessant nagging, lying, lack of respect, etc. If the physical and emotional requirements of both partners in a relationship are not met, the relationship will fail and only deteriorate.

However, what if you were the one excluded from the relationship? What if you had no warning whatsoever? What if you still care for your former partner? What if you were ignorant that your actions caused him or her to be unhappy in the relationship? What if you repeatedly harm them? What if all you want is their acceptance back?

There are so many hypotheticals.

When attempting to gain your ex back, you must first ask yourself, "What went wrong?" It can be difficult to admit that the relationship may have ended due to a mistake you made. Next, you should acknowledge your error before extending an apology. Prior to approaching your ex and begging them to return, you must confront your own demons.

When you were courting, did you lie? Do you lie? Have you been violent? Or perhaps you do not respect and treat them kindly; in that case, how do they deserve to be treated? Are you willing to change everything to preserve your relationship? Even if you mean it, it's too easy to say "I'm sorry," because the real objective is to be forgiven.

It is one thing to apologize, but quite another to truly apologize. It is beneficial to demonstrate to your ex that you have evolved, but you must first convince yourself. Whether you are genuine or not, your ex will know.

Find out why your poor behavior in the past caused the relationship to end by digging deep. Why did you begin to be abusive, dishonest, or dishonest? Work on self-improvement once you've identified the solution. You cannot be genuinely content in a relationship if you are unhappy with yourself.

Once you have resolved your own issues, you can ask your ex-partner for another chance with confidence.

Demonstrate that you will not continue the behaviors that led to the separation.

Even the best relationships can sometimes fail, which is a tragic and regrettable occurrence for most couples, but there is usually a reason, even if we don't always recognize it.

There are a number of factors that contribute to the demise of joyful partnerships. You may have endured futile disagreements or recently discovered that your ex cut off all communication before withdrawing, leaving you in the dark about what has been happening.

People who are in pain and unsure of where their partner stands in the relationship frequently act in the exact opposite manner in an attempt to gain back their ex.

This is so that men will act in ways that make sense to males and women will employ strategies that they find appealing. Learning that men and women think differently is crucial for maintaining a relationship and reconciling with an ex. Using masculine logic to try to win back a woman is typically ineffective, whereas the converse is true when attempting to win back a woman.

The truly tragic aspect of this is that despite their best efforts, both men and women in these situations have a tendency to act in ways that inadvertently and unintentionally alienate and push away the person they truly want back in their lives.

This indicates that they frequently act in the exact opposite manner that they should in order to win back their partner and reintegrate them into their lives, while remaining completely unaware of it. Think about this. Are your efforts to reunite with your ex bearing fruit? Or does it simply drive a wedge between you and that person, making you feel worse than you already do?

Let's examine what men and women contemplate in relationships, as well as how they interpret the behavior of their partners. Frequently, these revelations lead to a deeper understanding of what went wrong in the relationship and a greater awareness of what to do when beneficial relationships fail.

The biology of males and women is dissimilar.

In spite of the fact that it may seem redundant to state the obvious, there are significant hormonal and other biological differences that distinguish us from one another.

Did you know, for instance, that men frequently pursue testosterone-boosting methods in order to reduce their stress levels? They will thus monitor the news when they return home in order to discover ways to initiate their own "fix it" mentality after a challenging day. This suggests that they may enjoy resolving the problems of others because it motivates them to seek solutions. Even though he may be sitting quietly on the sofa, he may be contemplating this. As he manages his own tension levels, he will be unable to assist with real-world issues.

They will feel marginally happier after their testosterone levels rise, but they won't attempt to solve their own problems until they have sufficiently calmed down after a long day of trying to prove to their loved ones that they are a wonderful provider.

Unfortunately, women and men have fundamentally distinct biological impulses, which can cause difficulties in romantic relationships. For instance, when a woman's body contains more testosterone, she may feel more stressed and be inclined to dispute over trivial matters that her partner is unlikely to comprehend.

Women will learn how to produce oxytocin in order to reduce their tension levels. Oddly, oxytocin is known as the "cuddle hormone" in non-scientific circles and has been associated with maternal behavior in addition to being the bond formation hormone that causes a woman to seek a more intimate relationship with her partner.

In order to produce oxytocin, women must now feel cherished, adored, and valued. When they perceive that their partner is withdrawing from them for whatever reason, rather than the hormone testosterone saturating their system, their stress levels rise and they may become defensive.

When a man's testosterone levels decrease, he also experiences an increase in stress and an increase in his defensiveness. Interesting stuff, huh?

How Hormones Can Destroy a Wonderful Relationship

If you are a woman, you would have spent the day engaging in self-confidence-boosting or stress-relieving activities. You may have spent some time chatting with your companions about your various problems in order to reduce your stress, thereby increasing your oxytocin levels. You must have felt fantastic! However, this is not true for males.

Consider times when you were in a positive mood and eager to see your significant other. After a lengthy day of work, your ex-partner would have been exhausted and tense. Since discussing his problems causes his hormone levels to rise with the incorrect hormone, he has no desire to do so. While viewing television, he merely desires to unwind and perhaps devote a few minutes to resolving global problems.

Now, however, when his stress levels are elevated and perhaps intolerable, he is confronted by a partner who desires communication, sharing, cuddling, and affection. Now that he hasn't had time to decompress from his own hectic day, he must deal with a spouse who appears to be in excellent health but has no comprehension of his needs. Even though this is a simple example, can you see the problem? If there is a lack of awareness regarding these fundamental hormonal differences between men and women, even the best relationships may be destroyed.

Obviously, relationship dissatisfaction and relationship failure can occur for a variety of reasons.

5. Ignore Others and Adhere to Your Own Mantra

You know what to avoid doing. However, do you know what you should do? The objective is to make them regret their separation and lure them in. You will not implore your ex to return, but they will feel compelled to do so! The objective is to convince your ex that leaving you was a grave error. Such is the ideal!

How can you demonstrate your ex's regret?

- Direct communication: some individuals are just lucky. If your ex simply approaches you and says he or she misses you, you have won the conflict! You do not need to devise a devious strategy to gain back your ex.

- Indirect communication: this form of communication can be somewhat challenging. If your ex texts "I miss you," you can be certain that he or she regrets breaking up with you and likely wants to restart the relationship. There are more subtle indications your ex can drop on you, such as "I enjoy speaking with you" or "I prefer you to my new partner." You must recognize the subtle indications your ex is attempting to convey. These are indications that your ex desires the same thing you do: a reconciliation.

- Reliving old memories: presume you and your ex are still in communication. Whenever you two communicate, your ex-partner conjures up fond memories. This is evidence that your ex laments his or her previous lifestyle. Your ex is willing to resume a romantic relationship with you; otherwise, why would he or she continually bring up the past?

• Curious about your current life: If your ex has a keen interest in your life and asks you frequently about your dating life, it's possible that he or she regrets breaking up with you. Ensure that your ex is concerned about your decision to move on.

In contrast, not everyone is so fortunate. There are some obstinate ex-boyfriends and ex-girlfriends. If your ex left you because he or she believed he or she could find a superior catch, you must induce regret in him or her. You must recognize that the romance in a long-term relationship can wane over time. You must ensure that your ex constantly compares their next potential partner to you. Until he or she experiences adversity, he or she will be oblivious to how wonderful you guys had it. Thus, I deplore how you will draw your ex back to yourself.

What should you do to make your ex regret their decision? You will need to exert some effort, then. People are always so focused on their plans and schemes that they neglect to work on themselves. That will not occur. Make the initiative yourself. You will essentially need to demonstrate to your ex that you have moved on. In actuality, however, you have not. You must transform yourself into a fantasy. That is, you will have to transform into someone your ex will regret losing. Humans are drawn to objects that are both beautiful and intelligent. You should not be surprised by this. It is fundamental human nature! Consider that your ex has the option to choose between two attractive individuals. However, one is extremely intellectual while the other is less so. Which do you believe they will choose for a long-term commitment?

You must develop an aura that compels your ex to desire you. You must become accessible to him or her without becoming absolutely attainable. Do you get it? You must instill in your ex the fear that there is a very good possibility they will not get you back! Your ex must believe that you've outgrown him or her, when in fact you're longing to get back together.

You're Either Getting Better Or You Getting Worse

This is one of my favorite chapters because I believe many people neglect this topic. The majority of us are in a situation where we go to work, return home, then go to work and return home again. Most of us are in a robotic state, and we neglect that the most important thing is to improve ourselves and grow as individuals. I believe that because many individuals fail to work on themselves, their relationships become stagnant. Considering how nature operates, nothing stands still. You are either improving or deteriorating; there is no middle ground. Have you ever witnessed a long-term relationship in which the partners appear to lack affection for one another? In the beginning of a relationship, everything was new and exciting, and the couple could not get enough of each other. As the years past, neither of them improved as individuals; in fact, they began to regress. The early activities of their relationship are a distant memory. They provide justifications such as "were married" or "we've been together for a while, I no longer have to do those things." If you are no longer willing to devote your all in a relationship, there is nowhere to go but down. I do not believe that the majority of society believes that aging is detrimental. I believe that if you devote at least a few minutes per day to improving yourself, you will be a completely different person in a few years.

YOU CAN EITHER WIN THE BATTLE OR THE WAR.

Do you feel as though you must always win an argument or be right? The majority of people find it extremely challenging to interact with someone who must always be correct and win every argument. If you have the mindset that you must win every argument, you will win the battle but lose the war. In other words, you will win the argument and feel good about yourself, but you will gradually drive your partner away. Now, I'm not suggesting that this is a pristine world; disagreements are inevitable. It is a natural aspect of life. I am saying that sometimes, for the sake of your relationship, you must let certain things go. Which is more important: always being correct or having a happy relationship? If you reflect back on the arguments you've had in the past, you'll likely conclude that the vast majority were not even worth your time. I've heard it said that one should not focus on trivial matters in life.

You can communicate life or destruction There is a proverb that goes, "Sticks and stones may break my bones, but names will never hurt me." I believe that this is the furthest thing from the truth; names can be hurtful. Conflicts have been sparked by the use of negative language. Your words may communicate either life or death. Consider for a moment a few of the phrases you frequently use when conversing with your spouse. Do you believe that the majority of the time, your words to each other have been negative or positive? I believe that a relationship will rapidly deteriorate if negative words are frequently exchanged.

IMPORTANT THINGS YOU SHOULD NOT DO TO GET BACK WITH YOUR EX

- Stop sabotaging your chances with neediness, insecurity, and desperation • Halt all communication with your ex-partner. Give Your Ex-Partner What They Requested. A Breakup.

• Strive to Become a Person of Whom You Can Be Proud During No Contact. Someone Your Ex-Lover Cannot Resist.

• Contact Your Ex at the Appropriate Time with the Appropriate Message (Hint: Think Elephant) • Meet with Your Ex to Build Attraction, Connection, and Trust.

But what are these flaws you keep mentioning?
I'm glad you inquired because the first section of this article specifically addresses these issues.

Stop Ruining Your Chances with Neediness, Insecurity, and Desperation by Avoiding These Deadly Errors (aka The inclinations) I refer to this section as "The Instincts" because all of these errors are a direct result of people following their inclinations.

The majority of this book's advice is counterintuitive, but it works.

When you read it, you will understand why and everything will make sense.
Therefore, let's begin by discussing the fatal errors you must avoid at all costs.

Mistake No. 1: Constantly Calling And Texting Them
Jordan, we broke up 8 days ago. Since then, I have sent him daily messages, but he rarely responds. I must contact him a hundred times before I receive a single response. I genuinely adore him and desire to be with him, but I do not comprehend his behavior. He told me he adored me, and then began acting in this manner.

This is the narrative of 95 percent of individuals who are attempting to win back their ex-boyfriend or ex-girlfriend. It is a grave error to constantly text and call your former. It is a grave mistake to contact them even once. Your instincts indicate that if you maintain contact with your ex, they will not neglect you and may return.

However, it does not operate in this manner. In reality, every time you call or text your ex, you are communicating that you are dependent and lonely without them. This desperation is unattractive and pushes your ex further away.

Your instinct leads you to believe that this will be the nature of your interaction with your ex.

In actuality, however, it goes something like this.
You must exercise extreme caution when imbibing in public. You may wind up calling your ex and embarrassing yourself. Therefore, whenever you go out imbibing, bring a friend who can prevent you from making this error.

How can I win back my ex if I do not contact or text them?

You should contact them in a manner that will rekindle their attraction to you.

In a subsequent section, I explain in detail how to accomplish this.

Second Error: Begging And Attempting To Use Pity

If pleading after a divorce is effective, no one will ever break up again. They chose to abandon you and are willing to endure your pleading and begging.

Whatever the reason for the breakup, it will not affect your pleading. The only result of imploring is that you will appear weak and insecure.

Similarly, your instincts will lead you to believe that if you simply demonstrate to your ex that you cannot exist without them (or that you are miserable without them), they will accept you back.

Your mental pattern becomes similar to
If he realizes how much I miss him, he would return.
I can win him back if he realizes that I could not continue my existence without him.

Again, your instincts are playing you for a fool.

No one takes their ex back out of pity, believe me. No one is attracted to a miserable person.
And even if your ex-partner returned due to this, do you want him or her to remain with you out of pity?

Or do you desire their respect and adoration?

An old study demonstrates conclusively that the majority of individuals would choose a secure partner over an insecure one.

If you take a deep breath and consider the situation, you will realize that anything that makes you appear vulnerable will only push your former away. Your ex will not be attracted to you or consider a reconciliation if you beg, send them frequent messages, or are generally dependent.

Third Error: Permit Others to Walk All Over You

Your instincts tell you that if you merely comply with your ex's demands, they will return. Your intuition will inform you that your needs, values, aspirations, and goals are irrelevant.

Your instincts will tell you that reuniting with your ex is the only thing that matters. And you will sacrifice anything for it.

You allowed your ex to bully you. You turn into a doormat. You agree to your ex's most ridiculous proposals. However, your intuition tells you it's okay. Because having your ex back in your life is all that matters.

Well, what can I say?

Accepting everything your ex-partner says will not bring them back. In actuality, it will only diminish your ex's respect for you.

How can anyone value you if you do not value yourself?

Nobody desires a relationship with someone they do not respect. And even if they do return, they will quickly realize they have no respect for you as a person and depart.

Research indicates that every functional relationship has boundaries. And if you lack boundaries and self-respect in your relationship, you will likely end up in a toxic one.

Even if you are able to get your ex back by being a doormat, the relationship will be toxic and will inevitably end again.

Fourth error: lavishing them with affection.
Your intuition tells you that your ex will return if they realize how much you adore and care for them. You only need to convince them that no one will ever love them as much as you do.

How could they reject you once they comprehend your love for them?

In reality, they are already aware of your affection, adoration, and concern for them. Nevertheless, they resolved to split up. The reasons for their breakup with you will not magically vanish just because you adore them. Affection will not convince them to alter their minds.

The more you suffocate them, the more entrapped they will feel. And that will only encourage them to flee as quickly as feasible.

Fifth Error: Panicking When Your Ex Starts Dating

The prospect of your ex-partner being with someone else is nauseating. However, it is not as terrible as we portray it to be. First, let's examine how your inclinations change when you discover that your ex is seeing another person.

If I don't act immediately, they will fall in love with this new person and forget all about me. I should go there and do everything against which this text cautions.

I am willing to attempt anything, including pleading, using pity, expressing my love, and agreeing to all their terms (being a doormat). And if they do not answer the door, I will stand outside all day and call and text them.

I must inform my ex that this new person is completely unsuitable for them and that they are making a grave error by being in a relationship with this (INSERT DEROGATIVE COMMENT).

If you haven't realized it by now, when you discover that your ex-partner is seeing someone new, your intuition and thoughts shift into panic mode. In most situations, stress causes you to perpetrate the aforementioned errors.
In actuality, your ex is unquestionably involved in a rebound relationship.

In addition, the majority of rebound relationships end sooner rather than later. Many individuals utilize rebound relationships as a means of coping with breakups. Fortunately, it is one of the least effective methods for moving on. Therefore, the fact that they are in a rebound relationship does not imply that they will ignore you and move on.

In actuality, it signifies the opposite. As long as they are in this rebound relationship, they are able to evade their sadness. It also implies that they will take longer to get over you.

Reconnecting relationship
A rebound relationship is comparable to smoking. It is not wholesome. It creates a deceptive impression of peace. And it ends when the flame is extinguished. (the sooner you smoke the faster it terminates).
The most important thing to do when your ex is in a rebound relationship is to maintain your composure.

Whatever happens, do not advise your ex to end their relationship with their recovery partners. Let them suggest it.

After breaking up with you, they have an enormous vacuum in their lives that they are attempting to fill with someone else.

In most cases, they will soon realize that a rebound relationship cannot fill the void, and they will end the relationship.

Mistake #6: Calling By Name And Anger

Name-calling one's ex out of anger or frustration is a common response for those who were acclimated to doing so during arguments. It is also typical that you both repeatedly warned each other to separate.

Name-calling will only diminish your ex's attraction to you. However, it is unclear whether you are still panicked and whether your inclinations are set to fight or flee.

If you used to verbally abuse each other or become enraged during fights or arguments, there is a good chance that your instinct will compel you to do so again after you are separated.

Your natural inclination is to presume that this is just another argument or dispute. And if you simply show your ex your anger, they will calm down and express a desire to reconcile.

In the same manner as when you both engaged in combat.
This seldom succeeds. If your ex is sincere about the separation, your anger will only convince them that breaking up with you was the correct choice.

Being angry will remind them of all the negative fights and arguments that eroded the foundation of your relationship over time.

It will remind them that the two of you don't comprehend each other and make them believe that you are not the right person for them.

If you can relate, now is a great opportunity to recognize and address any unhealthy habits you may have developed over the years.

Conflicts should not always result in physical altercations, rage, or name-calling. I strongly suggest you attempt to learn healthful communication. Read texts on communication, and if necessary, seek therapy. Consider obtaining relationship coaching if you feel lost or confused and need assistance determining what to do next.

Seventh Error: Preoccupation and Misinterpretation

Possibly the worst aspect of a horrible separation is the subsequent infatuation.

You are racking your brain for the most effective strategy to reunite with your ex as soon as feasible.

Your mind searches for a foolproof plan. It desires assurance that you will reconcile with your ex in the future.

It will pose concerns such as

"Will my ex come back?"

"Is my ex-boyfriend missing me?"

"Does he still love me?"

"What can I do to bring him back instantly?"

"Will she start dating someone already?"

She went on a date; does this mean the relationship is over?

"He appeared happy in an Instagram photo he posted; does this mean he's over me?"

"My ex-boyfriend added me on Snapchat. Does this imply he desires to return? Does he want me to make contact?

If you write down all the concerns that keep popping into your mind, you will discover that they are largely inconsequential.

It is difficult to determine the correct responses to these questions. No one knows the correct answers to these queries, including you.

They are all about your ex-partner's mental state. Unless they are an oracle, no one can know precisely what is going through your ex's mind or what will happen in the future.

It's a fact. Your ex desires that you gain them back in the proper manner. They simply do not believe that you can.

These questions are the result of your mind's attempt to complete an impossible task. A task assigned by your instinct to your intellect.

Imagine that your mind is a device that will attempt to find a solution to any problem you present it with. Now suppose that your inclinations direct your mind to carry out the following:

"Find a solution that guarantees I will get my ex back one hundred percent.

Ensure that I do not lose my ex-girlfriend at all costs. Determine this strategy as soon as feasible, as my ex-partner may move on. If you don't, it will be exceedingly difficult for me (and by extension YOU) to survive."

Do you see the problem?

Your anxieties and instincts require your intellect to find a way to influence someone's free will. And it lacks the necessary resources to do so. In addition, your impulses jeopardize your life.

It is not surprising that your mind is in overdrive.

These questions will not drive your ex away on their own. However, while your mind is in overdrive, it is prone to making mistakes.

The majority of the aforementioned flaws are the result of poor discernment brought on by lack of forethought and panic. The Journal of Neuroscience-published research illustrates how anxiety can impair decision-making.

If you are panicked, constantly anxious, and worried about your breakup, you are highly likely to make mistakes that push your former away and increase your anxiety.

For instance, if your ex contacts you, you can interpret this as a sign that they want to reconcile and begin discussing how much you still care for them.

If your ex informs you that they still have feelings for you, you may be tempted to deliver flowers and chocolate to their home, believing that this is the type of reconciliation story depicted in the movies.

If your ex posts a photo on social media with a person of the opposite gender, you may conclude that they are dating, causing you to become anxious and make all of the mistakes listed above.

If you find out that someone admired a photo of you on Instagram, you can assume that they want to sleep with you. You may become anxious, call them, and conduct in a dominant or insane manner.

The simplest way to avoid creating a false impression is to take no action for a time. Not until your mind has calmed down and there is no longer intense dread.

During this period, it is also prudent not to listen to your friends and family. Most people are unable to evaluate a breakup and determine the best course of action that will lead to regaining your ex's affection, despite their good intentions.

What If I Have Already Committed These Errors?

There is a good chance that you have already committed at least one of these mistakes since the breakup. After a divorce, even the most intelligent monks in the Himalayas and Harvard psychology instructors frequently make these mistakes.

It is comparable to humans attempting to adhere to something dear. Don't torment yourself with it.

The most important thing for you to do right now is to realize that committing these errors will not help you win him back and to cease doing so immediately. Proceed to the next phase of the strategy, which will repair all the damage you've caused thus far.

Stop contacting your ex-partner. Give yourself some time and space, and grant your ex's request. A Breakup.

If you've done online research on breakups and getting your partner back, you're aware of the no-contact rule.

THESE WILL ASSIST YOU IN WINNING THEM BACK AND MAKE YOU HAPPIER IN THE PROCESS.

Does everything seem too wonderful to be true? Here are five things you can do to make the most of the No Contact Rule, as well as what you can anticipate to gain as a result.

Understanding How to Achieve True Confidence

You may not recognize it yet, but you have many reasons to feel confident. You do not recognize this about yourself, but you must now embrace your great talents. When you adhere to the No Contact Rule, you give yourself the opportunity to discover your inner confidence. Even if the breakup or the relationship caused you to experience negative emotions at times, you will find the inner fortitude to overcome them.

Finding true conviction within yourself enables you to be a happier, healthier, and more balanced individual. You may have previously struggled with your self-image. Probably, you only cared about what your ex thought of you. So many of us struggle with what it means to feel good about ourselves, but when you have the opportunity to reflect, you realize that you are a fantastic individual. You begin to hold your head a little higher, you begin to appreciate what you see in the mirror, and this positive energy is almost perceptible.

In addition, you will discover that confidence is one of the most attractive characteristics a person can possess. Your ex becomes even more alluring because they are curious as to why you are abruptly so confident. You're not doing this for them, but when you feel good about who you are, you're more alluring. The combination of self-assurance and the ability to win back your ex without even attempting is a winning one.

When you have a positive self-image, it is to your advantage. This is also the type of trait that your ex will notice and be drawn to, so taking the time to achieve and embrace confidence is advantageous and will help you get your ex back without even attempting!

Begin by Working on Yourself

If you are genuinely adhering to the No Contact Rule, this helps to provide perspective. Taking a step back affords you the opportunity to start over or press the reset button. You have the rare opportunity to focus first and foremost on improving yourself. In addition to making you a better person, this allows you to become the person you wish to be.

Do not assume that this will go unnoticed, as your ex will be fascinated by your newly discovered fortitude and power. When you are focused on improving yourself, you tend to think less about your ex.

When the No Contact Rule is properly applied, your ex will be out of sight and out of mind. You will continue to think about them because you ultimately want them back, but you will do so in moderation and control. You are not imploring them to return to you; rather, you are focusing on becoming a better person.

When considering how to get your ex back, it probably seems counterintuitive to focus on yourself. You likely believe that you should devote more time to reaching out to them and remaining present in their presence. Ignore these impulses however, as they are incorrect.

Make this divorce about YOU, and you'll be successful. You will discover inner fortitude that you were unaware you possessed. You will ultimately gain back your ex, primarily because you did not pursue them. They will notice your introspection, so take advantage of the No Contact Rule and use this time to become a better, happier individual.

You are considering what YOU want, and not what others want. You are contemplating how to cultivate your assets and improve your weaknesses. If you are able to adhere to this, you will have the time to invest in bettering yourself, which will pay off in a number of ways in the long run, including making yourself irresistible to your ex!

Stop Encouraging Your Compulsive Behavior

Here is where you must be completely truthful, regardless of how difficult it may be. Were you a little obsessive in your behavior during previous breakups? Can you identify times when you came on too strong or tried too hard, if you really delve deep? Did your emotions get the best of you, causing you to exert excessive effort in an attempt to win back your ex? Now is the moment to end this cycle for good!

Obsessive behavior will not help you gain back your ex; in fact, the opposite is true. The harder you push, the more you "stalk," and the more you attempt to win your ex back with clever little strategies, the further you push them away. If you want to win them back permanently, you must give them space and let them do the work, despite the fact that it may go against everything you think you know and believe.

The No Contact Rule is initially difficult to implement, but ultimately places you in control. It enables you to permanently cease your obsessive and unproductive behavior. It ensures that you overcome the undesirable patterns and conduct for which you are likely embarrassed.

This is a difficult part of the process for us because we do not want to acknowledge our past errors. We do not wish to acknowledge that we have obsessive traits or destructive behaviors. Simply accept responsibility, recognize that you've learned something from it, and move on. The No Contact Rule affords you the opportunity to reflect on your past actions. It also affords you the chance to ensure that you will never do it again; therefore, seize the opportunity, identify the obsessive behavior you once exhibited, and ensure that it remains in the past.

Work through the issues, frustration, and anguish of your breakup on your own, and give yourself the opportunity to stop feeding and using this obsessive behavior! The No Contact Rule will allow you to gain perspective and put an end to the behavior that has been stoking some troubling patterns.

Proceed with Your Life and Allow Them to Witness This

When someone tells you to move on, you likely become angry. When someone tells you that there are other fish in the sea or that you have it better than others, you likely disregard them.

The reality is, however, that if you refrain from contacting your ex for a month, you have the chance to move on with your life. Even though you will eventually want them back, you will discover that you no longer NEED them to breathe.

The No Contact Rule ensures you have the opportunity to move on and discover pleasure in other ways. It demonstrates that there is more to life than this individual, and you may even rediscover old acquaintances or your previous existence. Move on NOT FOR your ex, but FOR yourself. There is a distinction because you are not doing this to make your ex envious. You are doing this for a change to make yourself joyful.

You are permitted to begin having pleasure and experiencing joy in ways apart from this one person. In the long run, you realize that they are not the center of your universe and that you can move on and have a life without them.

Guess what happens when this capacity is increased? They are becoming aware! They see the pictures you post online of yourself doing interesting things. They observe that you actually appear joyful or content, and that your life is progressing without them. They disapprove of this in an instant! You demonstrate to yourself that you can move on and that existence consists of more than one person.

If you are able to gain them back, this is a tremendous benefit, but you are no longer desperate for their attention. Your ex recognizes your newfound independence, which motivates them to fight harder for you.

They desire to be a part of your existence and to be the source of your happiness. Even if they are unaware that this sparks something within them, when they see you moving on, they become significantly more motivated to put in the effort to gain you back. Works like a charm, and you discover some wonderful facets of your life along the way!

Allow Them to Lead for a Change

You're adhering to the No Contact Rule, and although it's initially difficult, you begin to appreciate its benefits. You begin to notice that your ex is gradually emerging from hiding. What seemed like a hiatus that would last forever is beginning to feel like a second chance. It's not that you don't miss your ex or want them back, but you discover that you're willing and able to let them take the initiative.

Your ex may view the Instagram photos you post of yourself doing interesting things. They may learn from shared acquaintances that you are doing well. This secretly drives them crazy! They likely mourn you as well, but they are more concerned with your ability to move on without them. This evokes emotions in them that they were previously unaware of. They want to see what this newfound confidence or contentment is all about and return to your life immediately.

You probably won't believe it at first, but you'll soon discover that your ex will contact you unexpectedly. They may call or text you or find some other pretext to contact you, even if it is a lame one. Suddenly, they appear extremely eager to see you, speak with you, or reintegrate themselves into your daily life. You may be surprised to discover that the No Contact Rule functions so well. You may find it hard to believe that your ex is actively pursuing you after a bad breakup, but it is possible, and you'll adore the results!

Your ex will take the initiative because they are more interested than you are. You have committed to the No Contact Rule, and as you approach the conclusion of this period, you will realize that they can no longer help themselves. They must see for themselves how pleased you are. They intend to make an effort to have you return.

They will pursue you and even attempt to obtain face-to-face interaction. At this point, you will realize that everything worked, and that your month of no contact with your ex gave you a real opportunity to win them back. All of this occurred without any effort on your part, which feels wonderful for a change!

www.ingramcontent.com/pod-product-compliance
Lightning Source LLC
Chambersburg PA
CBHW050232120526
44590CB00016B/2050